SPORTS INJURIES:
HOW TO PREVENT, DIAGNOSE, & TREAT

VOLLEYBALL

Sports Injuries:
How to Prevent, Diagnose, & Treat

- Baseball
- Basketball
- Cheerleading
- Equestrian
- Extreme Sports
- Field
- Field Hockey
- Football
- Gymnastics
- Hockey
- Ice Skating
- Lacrosse
- Soccer
- Track
- Volleyball
- Weight Training
- Wrestling

SPORTS INJURIES:
HOW TO PREVENT, DIAGNOSE, & TREAT

VOLLEYBALL

CHRIS BEESON

MASON CREST PUBLISHERS
www.masoncrest.com

Mason Crest Publishers Inc.
370 Reed Road
Broomall, PA 19008
(866) MCP-BOOK (toll free)
www.masoncrest.com

2 3 4 5 6 7 8 9 10

Beeson, Chris.
Volleyball / author, Chris Beeson.
p. cm. — (Sports Injuries)
Summary Recounts the history, rules and equipment of volleyball, physical and mental preparation required, common injuries, and how to pursue a career in volleyball.
Includes bibliographical references and index.

ISBN 1-59084-640-0 (hard : alk. paper)
1. Volleyball—Juvenile literature. 2. Volleyball players—Wounds and injuries—Juvenile literature. [1. Volleyball. 2. Sports injuries.] I. Title. II. Series.
GV1015.34.B44 2004
2003014702

Project Editor: Michael Spilling
Design: Graham Curd
Picture Research: Natasha Jones

Printed and bound in the Hashemite Kingdom of Jordan

PICTURE CREDITS
Corbis: 6, 8, 10, 12, 13, 19, 22, 23, 28, 30, 34, 44, 47, 54, 56, 57, 58;
©EMPICS: 15, 20, 26, 27, 33, 37; **Topham Picturepoint**: 17, 25, 38, 41, 43.

FRONT COVER: ©EMPICS (tr, tl); Corbis (br, bl).

ILLUSTRATIONS: Courtesy of Amber Books except:
Bright Star Publishing plc: 46, 49.

CONTENTS

Foreword

Sports Injuries: How to Prevent, Diagnose, and Treat is a seventeen-volume series written for young people who are interested in learning about various sports and how to participate in them safely. Each volume examines the history of the sport and the rules of play; it also acts as a guide for prevention and treatment of injuries, and includes instruction on stretching, warming up, and strength training, all of which can help players avoid the most common musculoskeletal injuries. *Sports Injuries* offers ways for readers to improve their performance and gain more enjoyment from playing sports, and young athletes will find these volumes informative and helpful in their pursuit of excellence.

Sports medicine professionals assigned to a sport that they are not familiar with can also benefit from this series. For example, a football athletic trainer may need to provide medical care for a local gymnastics meet. Although the emergency medical principles and action plan would remain the same, the athletic trainer could provide better care for the gymnasts after reading a simple overview of the principles of gymnastics in *Sports Injuries*.

Although these books offer an overview, they are not intended to be comprehensive in the recognition and management of sports injuries. The text helps the reader appreciate and gain awareness of the common injuries possible during participation in sports. Reference material and directed readings are provided for those who want to delve further into the subject.

Written in a direct and easily accessible style, *Sports Injuries* is an enjoyable series that will help young people learn about sports and sports medicine.

Susan Saliba, Ph.D., National Athletic Trainers' Association Education Council

Danielle Scott of the United States tries to spike through a Brazilian block at the 2000 Olympic Games in Sydney.

History

Volleyball is a game played in over 130 countries. Indeed, the *Fédération Internationale de Volleyball* estimates that more than 800 million people around the world enjoy bumping, setting, and spiking at least once a week. Yet the world's most popular team sport is little more than 100 years old.

Today, in the United States, volleyball is played at least once a year by nearly 25 million people, making it one of the top ten team sports. It is most popular among those twelve to seventeen years of age, with slightly more girls than boys taking part. Since the turn of the millennium, the sport has boosted its followers by nearly 20 percent. Fun, fast, and growing, this successful game was born in the United States, in the state of Massachusetts. William G. Morgan (1870–1942), who created the game in 1895, was studying as an undergraduate at the YMCA's Springfield College when he met James Naismith. In 1891, Naismith had invented basketball, and Morgan saw how much that game was enjoyed by the students. After graduation, Morgan took up the post of Director of Physical Education at the YMCA at Holyoke, Massachusetts. There he established a program of exercises, and his enthusiasm made his classes a great success. Still, he wanted more variety in his program, and for that he needed a team sport.

Morgan thought back to how popular Naismith's game had been in Springfield, and he saw great potential in basketball. However, to broaden the range of people

Volleyball has come a long way since its invention in Massachusetts in 1895, but the game's emphasis on fitness and fun has never changed.

who could participate, he needed game that was a little less physically combative. So Morgan invented a game he called "mintonette." It required a range of physical and tactical skills, similar to basketball, but was not as rough, and was therefore open to many more people. When inventing the rules of mintonette, Morgan took much of his inspiration from tennis and handball. Mintonette required a net 6 feet 6 inches (1.98 m) high; a court 50 x 25 feet (15.2 x 7.6 m), indoors ideally; and any number of players divided into two teams.

A match involved nine innings, with each team making three **serves** per inning. As in tennis, the server was allowed two serves to get the ball into the opposition

Simple rules and minimal equipment helped volleyball to become one of the world's most popular team sports.

court, and, after the ball had been successfully served, hitting the net meant a side-out (losing serve) or a point lost. Each team could pass the ball between themselves any number of times before hitting it into the opposition court.

The sport caught on quickly, unlike the name mintonette. During a demonstration match at the Springfield YMCA in 1896, a spectator observed to Morgan that the aim of the game was to volley the ball over the net. Morgan changed the sport's name to volleyball, and its increasing popularity supported this change.

In 1900, after some years of competition, W.E. Day (a colleague of Morgan's) revised the rules. The height of the net was raised by 1 foot (30 cm) to 7 feet 6 inches (2.28 m), the number of players was limited to sixteen per team, and matches were to be played to 21 points. But the most significant change was the introduction of a ball designed specifically for the sport. Volleyball's popularity soared in the United States, and then began to spread around the world.

VOLLEYBALL GOES WORLDWIDE

In 1906, the sport was played in Cuba after U.S. army officer Agusto York arranged a match there. In 1908, it reached Japan in the hands of Hyozo Omori, a Springfield YMCA graduate. Max Exner and Howard Crokner took the sport to China in 1910. Elwood Brown, YMCA Director in Manila, introduced the sport in the Philippines. Within a few years, there were 5,000 courts throughout that country. In 1914, volleyball was drafted into the military when Dr. George J. Fisher, secretary of the YMCA War Office, introduced the game as part of a fitness program for the American armed forces. During World War I, it was played by both American and British servicemen, and its popularity spread throughout Europe and into Africa. In 1922, the rule specifying three consecutive hits per team emerged. Later that year, the United States hosted the first national volleyball championship, contested by YMCA teams from all around the country. The game became truly international in 1935, when the first official international volleyball matches took place: the U.S.S.R. (the Union of Soviet Socialist Republics, now collapsed) played Afghanistan in Tashkent and Moscow.

In April 1947, the sport's governing body, the *Fédération Internationale de Volleyball* (**FIVB**), was formed. The FIVB brought together fourteen national authorities under the leadership of France's Paul Libaud. Through harmonization of American and European rules, the court dimensions were defined as 59 feet x 29 feet 6 inches (18 x 9 m) with a net height of 7 feet $11^5/_8$ inches (2.43 m) for men and 7 feet $4^1/_8$ inches (2.24 m) for women—dimensions that still stand today.

Students at Los Angeles City College enjoying the game in 1941. By this time, U.S. troops stationed around the world were also playing volleyball.

World championships

With a world governing body in place, volleyball became more organized globally. In 1948, Czechoslovakia won the first European championships, which were held in Rome. The following year, the U.S.S.R. won the first men's world championships, in Prague. In 1952, the women of the U.S.S.R. matched their men by winning the first women's world championship before a home crowd in Moscow. Attendance at these early world championships was sparse, and it

Rival teams play volleyball during an informal tournament in Malatapay, on the Philippine island of Negros.

was not until 1956 that a truly comprehensive world-class event was hosted, in Paris. With the game now established as a genuinely international sport, volleyball took its first official steps onto the Olympic stage. Huge tactical steps forward were made as teams vied for gold: the **forearm pass** (**bump**), soft **spike** (**dink**), and defensive diving all developed during this time. In 1964, the first Olympic gold medals were won by the U.S.S.R. (the men's event) and Japan (the women's event). The sport has been a regular feature of the Olympics ever since.

Volleyball became increasingly popular with professional athletes. In 1990, the first World League for men was formed, with a prize of $1 million for the winning nation. In 1992, this figure rose to $3 million; in 1996, $6 million. The Grand Prix, the World League for women, was established in 1993.

THE RULES OF INDOOR VOLLEYBALL

Indoor volleyball is a game played by two teams of six players on a court bisected by a net. The aim is to use your hands and arms to send the ball over the net, grounding the ball in your opponent's court and avoiding the ball being grounded in your own. The back right player serves the ball over the net into the opponent's court and the receiving team has three hits, not including blocks, to return the ball over the net. Players cannot hit the ball twice in succession, unless the first hit is a block.

The rally continues until the ball grounds or goes "out," landing beyond the lines that define the playing area. A rally also stops if the ball is not returned within three hits, or if one team commits a foul. Winning a rally means that the team receives a point and then serves again. If the receiving team wins the rally, they receive a point and the right to serve, and their team **rotates** one position clockwise.

Volleyball matches are played over three or five games. Non-deciding games are played to 25 points, and the winning team must gain a clear two-point advantage

BEACH VOLLEYBALL

The sport has never forgotten its roots—to promote fitness and fun—and in warmer climates, it was not long before a more acrobatic version of the game was being played on beaches. The earliest records show that beach volleyball was being played in the 1920s on the beach at Santa Monica, between teams of six. By 1930, the sport was being played by teams of two players, but it was not until 1948 that the first official tournament was held,

Australia's Sarah Stratton recovers from a dive in a match against the United States during the 2000 Olympic Games in Sydney.

on the beach at Los Angeles. The prize was a case of Pepsi-Cola. In the 1950s, tournaments were played wherever there was a beach.

The California Beach Volleyball Association (CBVA) was set up to regulate the sport in 1965, and volleyball's obvious appeal attracted big-money sponsors. The FIVB was quick to formalize beach volleyball, featuring two-player teams, and the first world championships were held in 1987 in Brazil. In 1989, the beach volleyball World Series was established, and in 1996, beach volleyball made its Olympic debut.

(25–23, 26–24, 27–25). Deciding games (the third or the fifth) are played to 15 points, the winning team gaining a clear two-point advantage. There is no points cap in either case.

The players

Players must know and observe the rules, and accept the referees' decisions as final, doing so in a sporting way (although the team captain—but only the captain—may request clarification of a decision). Attempting to deceive officials or delay the game is not allowed. Players may talk to each other during the game and coaches can direct from off court without disturbing or delaying the match.

THE COURT

The court is divided into functional areas by lines at least 2 inches (5 cm) wide. These areas are:

- boundary lines—two along the sides and two at each end, marking the playing area's extremities.
- center line—one across the middle of the court, below the net, splitting it into two team zones, both 29 feet 6 inches x 29 feet 6 inches (9 x 9 m).
- attack lines—these mark the front zones in each court and lie 9 feet 10 inches (3 m) from the center line.
- service zone—this extends at least 6 feet 6 inches (2 m) and, at most, 29 feet 6 inches (9 m) behind the end line, and is limited laterally by two short extensions of the side boundary lines.

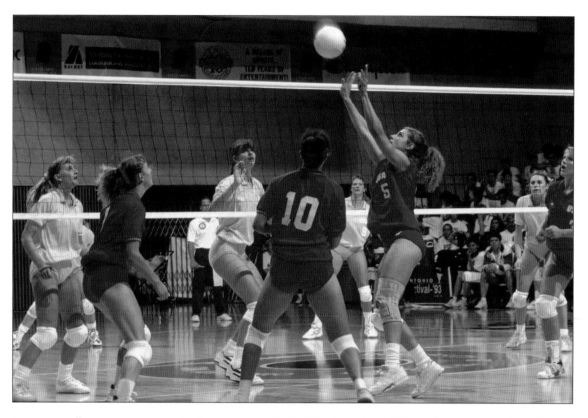

Here, two college teams compete in the women's volleyball finals at the 1993 U.S. Olympic Festival, held in San Antonio, Texas.

There are six player positions. Before each serve, each player must be stationary in their position. The service position (back right) is position one; front right, position two; front center, position three; front left, position four; back left, position five; and back center, position six. After the ball is served, players can move freely about the court.

After a team wins the right to serve, players rotate one position clockwise (one moves to six, two to one, three to two, and so on). The players' order is specified by the coach and agreed to by the match officials, and it cannot be changed unless it is by **substitution**.

THE RULES OF BEACH VOLLEYBALL

Beach volleyball is, as you would expect, very similar to indoor volleyball, but there are a few key differences. The sport can be played competitively by two-, three-, four-, or six-player teams, same-sex or mixed, and only for a team of six players is rotation or position relevant. There are two formats for play. The first is a one-game match, which is won by the first team to reach thirty points with a two-point advantage. The second is won by the best of three games. The first two games are played to twenty-one points with a two-point advantage and the deciding game is played to fifteen points, again with a two-point advantage.

A block counts as a hit and each side is limited to three consecutive hits. The net should never be touched, and players may use any part of their body to play the ball, except at serve. There is also a play known as a joust, where two players both have their hands on the ball at the net.

THE COURT

Beach volleyball can be played on grass or sand, and the surface must be safe for players. For the two-player team game, the court is 52 ft 6 in x 26 ft 3 in (16 x 8 m), but for three-, four-, and six-player teams, the court is the same size as the indoor court. All have the same net height.

THE BALL

This is the same as its indoor cousin except for the pressure. A beach volleyball must be inflated to 2.5–3.2 lb/in^2 (175–255 g/cm^2).

A player leaps to power a serve at a pro beach volleyball tournament in Belmar, New Jersey.

Fit Body, Fit Mind

To compete as well as you want to and stay as fit as you need to, you must condition the mind as well as the body. If you are not relaxed enough to concentrate fully on what is required of you—to focus on the game and your role in the team—you will be less effective as a player and more susceptible to injury.

There are many different methods for taking control of your own mind, and you should explore these options to find which method works best for you. Some people listen to loud music, others prefer silence. Some use deep breathing, others close their eyes and try to concentrate on a single point, finding that the concentration required helps them to clear their minds. Apart from the techniques already mentioned, stretching and yoga are useful ways of warming up, and both release muscle tension. Any of these methods will help lessen your anxiety about the game and its importance to you and your team. Rather, they will help you focus on what is really important: your performance individually and as a team player.

Once you have released the anxiety that clouded your mind and prevented you from gaining focus, use mental rehearsal to prepare for your performance. Think about your duties on the court and how you have been coached to play. Recall what you used to do wrong and what steps you took to correct those mistakes. Think of the last time you performed well. What set that performance apart? What made the difference? That is what you need to succeed.

Brazilian captain Nalbert Bitencourt holds up the volleyball World Cup in celebration with teammates, after beating Russia in the 2002 final in Argentina.

Think of the directions given by your coach, with particular focus on any new plays. Run through those plays in your head, using different angles to improve your visualization. Where did the play go wrong in training? How do you avoid getting the play wrong? If the play goes wrong again, what steps can you take to retrieve the situation? And having returned the ball, what defensive formation do you need to take up? Who do your opponents have at the net and what are they likely to do? Think your way through the game, and you will react much quicker on the court.

Most of us are guilty at times of getting a little too involved in our game. Sometimes the passion overpowers the play, and in our urge to spike the ball through the floor, we mess up. It is important for each of us to find our most productive level of arousal, in terms of performance. We must have enough adrenaline flowing in our blood to sharpen our eyes, ears, and reactions, but not so much that we lose control. It is essential that we strike a balance between

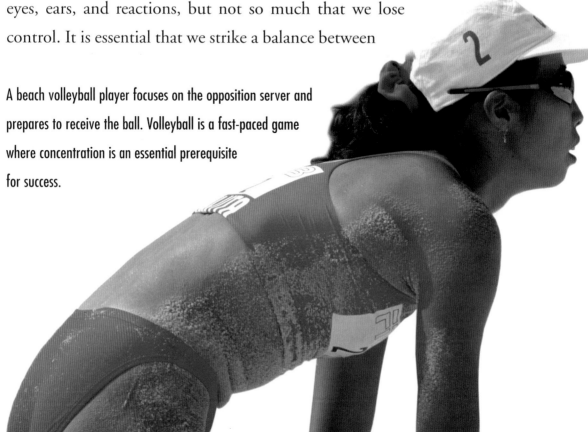

A beach volleyball player focuses on the opposition server and prepares to receive the ball. Volleyball is a fast-paced game where concentration is an essential prerequisite for success.

SERVING

SERVING UNDERARM

- Stand facing the opposition court with the left foot forward.
- Hold the ball at waist height with the left hand and draw back the right arm. Simultaneously lean forward, placing your weight on your left foot, and swing the right arm toward the ball.
- Withdraw the left hand just before contact, hit the ball with the palm or heel of the right, then follow through with the right arm.

SERVING OVERARM

- Stand facing the opposition court with your left foot forward and the ball at chest level in your left hand. Raise and draw back your right arm.
- With your wrist stiff and your arm straight, toss the ball vertically 18–24 in (45–60 cm).
- Simultaneously lean forward, placing your weight on your left foot, then swing the right arm forward to hit the ball with the heel of the right hand, and follow through.

Nancy Reno of the United States prepares to serve overarm during an international beach volleyball tournament.

PASSING

READY PASSING POSITION

When preparing to receive the ball, stand with your feet spread, your knees bent, your hips over your ankles, your shoulders ahead of your knees, and your arms straight and at 90° to the torso.

PASSING

Forearm pass, when receiving a serve; dig (the same maneuver, but defensively), when receiving an attack:

- Position yourself to meet the ball straight on, using shuffle-steps (sideways steps) to cover ground.
- As the ball approaches you, draw your hands together and move the arms from the shoulder, keeping them straight.
- Contact the ball at hip level, just above the wrists and with your hands together, then follow through.
- If you want to change the direction of your return, make sure your follow through is in the direction you want the ball to go.

Practice passing with your teammates by standing in a circle and passing to each other. Give yourselves enough space to move to the ball.

the will and the skill required to perform. That balance is different for every player, and only you will know how to get to where you need to be.

If you are too hyped up, your muscles will be tense, lacking their usual flexibility.

Your coordination will not be as good as it should be, and you will be unable to focus your attention effectively. This means that you will be more prone to injuries, including muscle tears, sprains, and strains. If you lose a few points on the spin, it is especially important that you remain cool. Concentrate on getting the basics right, try to read your opponents' plays, and tell your teammates to calm down and take charge. Above all, don't lose your head. If your fear of failure is too great, you will be too emotional to perform. If you and your teammates panic, you have already lost.

SPORT FOR FITNESS AND FUN

Some students pursue sports in hope of getting a college scholarship or a place on a professional team. Statistically, the chances of landing a college scholarship are not great. This can have as much to do with where your school is located, the standard of coaching, and even the general level of athletic ability there, as it does with your personal performance and abilities.

Explore your potential by working hard, but never lose sight of the fact that sports—especially volleyball—are all about fitness and fun.

Accurate passing requires technique and concentration. This player is cushioning the ball for a colleague to hit over the net.

IMPROVING STEP BY STEP

While it would be unwise to beat yourself up over bad results such as losing a game, you should not ignore the experience either, or try to block it out. Instead, try turning that negative experience into a positive one by looking at your performance and figuring out how you could improve it. Ask your coach how you could improve your game and then, with your coach's advice, create a training strategy to address the improvements that you need to make. This is not a difficult step to take, but it is the first, and a very important one.

Cuba's Mireya Luis (no. 3), the best women's player ever, celebrates with her team during a match against the United States at the 1996 Olympic Games.

Your strategy should be made up of medium-term goals that are attainable and measurable. If being out of shape is your problem, set a goal to improve your level of fitness within a month. Run 400 yards (365 m), and record your time. Aim to reduce that time by a realistic margin, perhaps three to five percent, after a month's training. Do not push yourself too hard; set a goal you can reach.

Once you have achieved a goal, raise it again. Your goal should be to become a complete player, equally good at serving, setting, spiking, blocking, bumping, dinking, and diving. You will enjoy the results, your game will certainly improve, and you will inspire your teammates to play at a higher level, too.

DEFENSE

READY DEFENDING POSITION

- Stand with your feet spread, knees bent, hips back, shoulders forward, and your hands ahead of you, palms facing up.
- Try to remain still while digging the ball, and aim to dig the ball in an arc 20 feet (6 m) above the court, passing through the plane of the net cord about 3 feet (1 m) to your side of the net.

BLOCKING

- Keep your feet planted, ready to jump, and shoulders square to the net.
- Keep your hands a ball's width apart, thumbs vertical, fingers diagonal, and arms straight.

- When timing your jump, watch the setter to find out where the ball is heading.

  Once the hitter/spiker has been identified, watch his approach and see where his eyes are looking to indicate the direction of the hit. Then move to block it.

Bryan Ivie of the United States blocks an attack at the net during the 1996 Olympic Games in Atlanta.

Physical Preparation

Just as the mind requires preparation to raise its performance level, so does the body. Unless you warm up or do some form of stretching exercise, sudden bursts of activity are likely to cause injury. Your muscles, ligaments, and tendons will not be flexible enough to endure strenuous physical activity.

A warm-up and cool-down routine is essential, both before and after exercise. It is a good habit to develop and, when combined with your mental preparation, provides you with a pre game routine that will help you to focus your mind on the challenge ahead.

The warm-up is designed to limber up the body and prepare it for prolonged exertion. Wear an extra layer of clothing to hold in the warmth you generate, and keep this layer on until you are called onto the court for the game.

The ideal warm-up routine includes three distinct aspects: **aerobic**, stretch, and practice.

AEROBIC

The goal here is to raise the heart and respiration rates slowly. As you begin to breathe more quickly and deeply, your lungs take in more air. This, combined with your increasing heart rate, raises the level of oxygen in the blood. This helps your body to convert stored energy and increases the flow of blood throughout

With the right physical preparation, you can reduce the chance of injury and concentrate on enjoying the actual playing of volleyball.

the body. The increased heart rate also raises body temperature, warming and loosening the muscles and tendons.

Ten minutes of brisk walking or jogging will prepare your body, and it will also help you to clear your mind and focus on the game ahead. After this, try a few short on-the-spot sprints.

STRETCH

This section of the warm-up is designed to prepare your muscles, tendons, and ligaments for what lies ahead. While general stretches are important, be sure to also choose specific stretches that work on the muscle systems that you are about to use the most. For volleyball, this means the shoulders, back, groin, legs, knees, and ankles.

Hold each stretch for thirty seconds before release. Stretch steadily and gradually; don't bounce or pump the stretch position, as this could snap a tendon or ligament. Slowly extend the stretch up to, but not beyond, the point where you feel it begin to pull. Work on complementary areas—for instance, stretch your **quadriceps** for thirty seconds, and then stretch your **hamstrings** for thirty seconds. Stretch only as far

Every physical workout should begin with a warm-up and end with a cool-down.

As you grow older, stretching becomes more important, so it is a good habit to begin while you are still young.

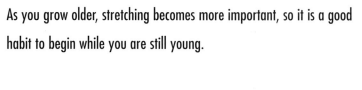

as you comfortably can, and pay specific attention to areas that have recently recovered from injury.

PRACTICE

This section is designed to help your body and mind get into competition mode. You go through all the different maneuvers your body will be performing, beginning with the most gentle:

- Start with triangle passing, an exercise to raise your perception and coordination. It will also stretch and warm your shoulders and limber up your hips, knees, and ankles. Stand in a triangle with two other teammates, and pass the ball between you. Do this for three to five minutes.
- Next, spend three to five minutes serving and returning alternately in pairs— not at full intensity, but building toward match level.
- Then spend three to five minutes setting, hitting, and blocking, again building in intensity.

By this stage, you should be prepared for the match, both physically and mentally. If there is any part of your body that is not ready for what lies ahead, you will find out about it during this warm-up. If so, consult your coach about whether you can play.

SETTING AND HITTING

SETTING

This sets up the ball for spiking and is also used as an overarm pass.

- Face the target with your left foot forward and your weight on the right foot, knees bent and feet spread.
- Raise your hands 6–8 inches (15–20 cm) ahead of your forehead as if cupping the ball, looking through the triangle made by your first fingers and thumbs, and keeping hands, forehead, and hips in a line.
- Just before you contact the ball, straighten your arms and legs while keeping your eye on the ball, then follow through in the direction you want the ball to go.
- For setting, your goal is to drop the ball just inside the sideline, 3 ft. (1 m.) to your side of the center line.

HITTING

This maneuver is used for attacking and spiking.

- If using a three- or four-step run-up, make sure your last step is the longest and most powerful. Plant your left foot, then swing both arms ahead of you and take off vertically with both feet slightly apart.
- Extend your left arm out ahead of you and draw the right arm back, above, and behind your shoulder with your right arm bent.
- Drop the left shoulder and then, keeping the right arm slightly bent, use the heel or palm of the right hand to make contact with the ball immediately above and ahead of the forehead.

Most of the injuries seen in volleyball occur at the net, where the game's action is at its hottest and contact between players is most likely. Here, France's Laurent Capet (right) jumps to volley the ball as Bulgaria's Evgeni Ivanov attempts to block in the 2002 World Cup tournament.

COOL-DOWN

After the match has finished, put on an extra layer of clothing so that you do not cool down too fast, which would mean that your soft muscle tissue would become sore and stiff. Slow your body down by jogging gently for five minutes, then finish off with ten minutes of stretching, paying particular attention to the areas you have exerted most.

Equipment and Accessories

Like any sport, volleyball requires its players to have some basic equipment in order to play the game safely. For example, a good pair of shoes and knee pads are essential for the indoor game. For beach volleyball, a hat and sunscreen should be at the top of the list.

The list of equipment you must have for volleyball is quite short, but there is an ever-widening range of equipment and accessories on the market. What is it for, and do you need it?

BASIC INDOOR EQUIPMENT
Shoes

A good pair of shoes is the first priority. The brand and model is not nearly as important as that the shoes are reasonably new and fit well.

Shoes age relatively slowly, so you may not notice the slight reduction in spring and support as the months slip by. Many players complaining of knee problems, however, buy new shoes and find their problems significantly reduced. Volleyball is a sport that places great demands on footwear: players need shoes that have a high-grip sole, and that can cope with takeoffs, landings, and sudden changes of

Nancy Reno (facing, wearing sunglasses) of the United States women's team is seen here in action at the net during an international beach volleyball tournament.

ARCH SUPPORTS AND HEEL CUSHIONS

If you find that you are experiencing knee problems, even with new shoes, you should ask about arch supports. If your feet tend toward overpronation and roll inward, your kneecap will not move smoothly in its groove. This is what causes much of the knee pain experienced by volleyball players. Arch supports correct overpronation and should ease any knee pain. If over-the-counter products do not help, consider having some custom-made.

Heel cushions are designed to help reduce compression throughout the leg during landing, but a good pair of shoes should give you all the shock absorption that you need. If you do find yourself landing heavily on your heels during a game, work on building up your calves and improving your balance.

direction. All of these combine to shorten the life of a pair of volleyball shoes. Make sure that yours are up to the job.

When it comes to shoes, the importance of a good fit cannot be overstated. Your feet will be pounded side to side, up and down, and back and forth inside your shoes. If the shoes do not fit properly, they will cause trouble. If they are too big, your feet will slide around inside them, hampering your movement and slamming your toes into the front of the shoe. If they are too small, they will squash your feet as they heat up and expand during play, meaning that you could lose a toenail or two in the short term, and possibly suffer deformation in the long term.

Dan Landry of the United States dives to dig the ball during the 1996 Olympic Games in Atlanta.

Ankle braces and guards

For volleyball players, ankles are the most frequently injured parts of the body because of the speed of the game and the amount of jumping involved. If you injure your ankles often, and find the injuries are getting increasingly serious and recovery is taking longer each time, you may need to use an ankle brace. (Do not use tape strapping—it loses half its support after ten minutes.) You will also need to strengthen the ankle and increase its flexibility, but wearing an ankle brace will prevent the likelihood of further damage.

Wearing a brace also has psychological benefits. The brace will make you more aware of your ankle's position in space, and you will find yourself moving in a way that is less likely to result in injury. The brace will also help you mentally: rather than worrying about your ankle, you will be able to concentrate on your role in the team.

Most volleyball players will find themselves on the floor at some stage during a match, so protective equipment, such as knee pads, are essential accessories.

GENERAL SUPPORT

Volleyball played competitively provides a serious workout. Aches and pains are inevitable—although warming up and cooling down properly will keep them to a minimum. If you are feeling the effects of your workout, you may want to use some of the supports available in good sports stores.

Among the large variety available are Achilles tendon supports, hamstring supports, back supports, elbow supports, and shoulder supports. If you think that wearing one of these will make a difference in the way that you feel and play, or if your coach has recommended you buy one, you should do so. Or, you could adjust your training schedule and make sure that it includes a little more strengthening work in those areas. The results will be longer lasting.

Knee and elbow pads

Volleyball should be played on wooden floors—a surface that provides at least some give—rather than on concrete or linoleum. By diving for a ball, you could easily damage a kneecap, hip, elbow, or shoulder, which could cause a great deal of pain and keep you out of the game for months.

Knee braces, straps, and sleeves

There are several products on the market designed to offer support to the knee, but their effectiveness has yet to be proven. There are several classifications:

• functional—giving additional support for injured knees;

- rehabilitative—limiting movement of the knee while it heals;
- prophylactic—for protection from traumatic impact;
- patellofemoral—helping the kneecap (patella) move smoothly over the knee joint.

Of these, the functional and rehabilitative ones have been shown to be effective.

Some people, however, believe that wearing braces may acutally increase the likelihood of injury, either because this allows the athlete to overload a knee which is not strong enough to deal with the load or because the brace's external support structure serves to weaken the knee's own natural support structure. Most athletes who wear them, however, believe that they help, and that factor alone is important.

If you do decide to wear a knee support, it is important to make sure it fits correctly; otherwise, it is worse than useless. Also, you need to wear it whenever you are increasing the load on your knee, which means during warm-up, just as much as when training or playing a match. Remember, too, that your knee brace is the least important aspect of preventing knee injury, or of rehabilitation after knee injury. Stretching and strengthening the legs, and managing your fitness program correctly, are far more important.

Finger and wrist protection

Injuries to the hands and wrists are the third most common type of injury after those to the ankle and the knee—and you do not need a great deal of knowledge about volleyball to see why. Maneuvers such as the **floater** serve and the spike place great loads on the wrist, and throughout the course of a season, strains are not uncommon. Likewise, it is not unusual for fingers and thumbs to be sprained when blocking.

There are gloves and other products on the market to protect your hands, but strapping, applied correctly, will provide your fingers, thumbs, and wrists with the necessary support. If a finger is sprained, you can prevent further injury when training and playing by strapping it to the next finger—a procedure known as **buddy taping**. There are also finger braces on the market.

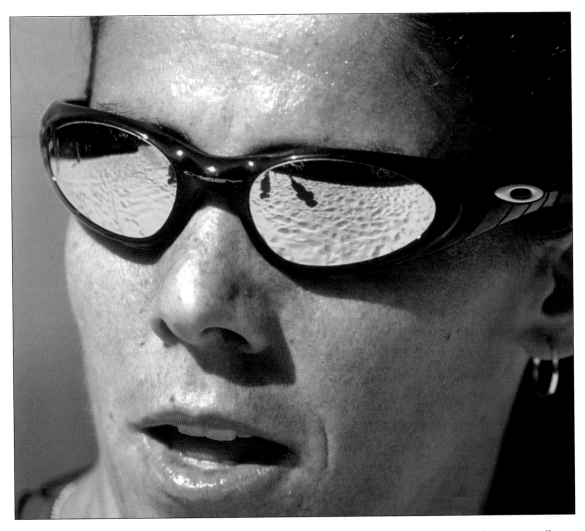

Good-quality sunglasses with UVA and UVB protection, broad-spectrum sunscreen, and plenty of water are all essentials for beach volleyball players.

EQUIPMENT FOR BEACH VOLLEYBALL

Sand is a much more forgiving surface to play on than wood and eliminates the need for shoes, kneepads, and elbow pads. It also reduces—but does not eliminate—the likelihood of ankle and knee injuries. Even so, the outdoor game includes one big danger that does not factor in the indoor game—the sun.

SUNSCREEN

Even on cloudy days, the sun's UV (ultraviolet) rays are strong enough to burn the skin. For this reason, it is essential that players, officials, and spectators wear a reliable, broad-spectrum sunscreen. Beach volleyball players spend a great deal of time on the sand, and failure to apply a protective layer of sunscreen will increase your risk of skin cancer.

HAT

Wearing a peaked, baseball-style hat will help to protect your face from the sun's UV rays. It will also help to keep the sun out of your eyes.

SUNGLASSES

It can be very difficult to see the ball without a good pair of sunglasses. Without them, sunlight—whether directly, glinting off the ocean, or reflecting off something shiny—can leave you with temporary blind spots. Make sure your sunglasses are also UVA and UVB resistant. Eyes, like skin, can burn: if your eyes are exposed to sunlight for as little as six hours without protection, they will feel gritty, and may begin to water profusely. These are symptoms of sun blindness, and the only cure is to keep your eyes cool and covered for eighteen hours.

FINGER AND WRIST PROTECTION

Beach volleyball players will find that their fingers, thumbs, and wrists take a battering. Strap or brace as you would for the indoor game.

The Brazilian women's beach volleyball team can be seen here preparing their attack during the 2000 Olympic Games in Sydney, Australia.

Common Injuries

Considering how fast-moving a sport volleyball is, injuries are surprisingly infrequent. At Olympic level, a volleyball player will suffer an injury after an average of twenty-five hours on the court; at national amateur level, after fifty hours. At this level, about half of all players can expect one injury during a season, though most injuries will be minor enough to allow resumed play within a week.

Jumping (or rather landing) in defense is responsible for most of the injuries seen in volleyball. Players have to jump when both attacking and defending. Blocking is also injurious as it can involve landing on the opposition's feet. Most hand injuries in volleyball are caused by blocking. The spike is the second most hazardous activity, again placing the ankle at risk. In both cases, jumping places great demands on the knee. The more volleyball that you play, the more likely it is that you will suffer from the single most common **overuse injury**: jumper's knee.

Broadly speaking, volleyball injuries fall into two categories: acute and overuse. An **acute injury** tends to be traumatic, caused by a single event such as a sprain, whereas overuse injuries become more of a problem as you spend more time on the court. Both of these types of injury are most likely to occur to the ankles, knees, hands, and wrists, with the ankle being particularly vulnerable.

With the right preparation, most injuries can be avoided, but the nature of volleyball does mean that some injuries are more likely than others.

ANKLE LIGAMENTS

The ankle is more likely to become injured than any other joint. Sprains occur when the ligaments are overextended and some or all of their component fibers tear.

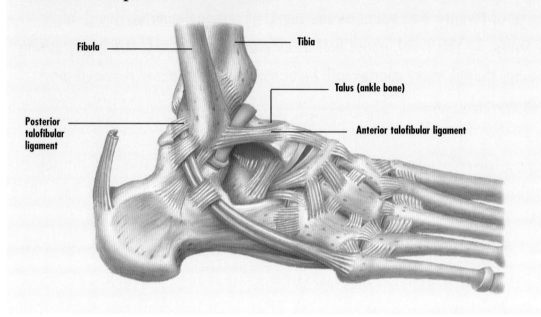

Fibula

Tibia

Talus (ankle bone)

Posterior talofibular ligament

Anterior talofibular ligament

ACUTE INJURIES
The ankle

Ankle injuries account for almost two-thirds of all acute injuries. Most result from jumping at the net, either to block or to spike. If a player lands slightly off balance, or her foot moves below the net and lands on an opponent's foot, the ankle may roll over onto the outside of the foot. This is known as forced supination, or **inversion**, and results in overextension of the ligaments—usually called a sprained ankle.

There are three degrees of sprain. If the talo-fibular ligaments have been stretched or slightly torn, but you can stand on the ankle without too much pain, you will feel only a slight swelling and stiffness in the ankle. For second-degree sprains, the tearing of the talo-fibular ligaments will be more significant, causing heavy swelling and more pain, leaving the ankle itself unstable and feeling very stiff. Third-degree sprains involve the complete rupture of the talo-fibular ligaments, leaving the ankle disabled, severely swollen, and extremely painful.

Hand injuries

Most hand injuries are the result of blocking attacks. These result in sprains of the fingers and thumbs. Depending on the injury, a player will be able to go back on court quickly, by using either buddy taping or thumb spica taping—where the thumb, wrist, and hand are taped for extra support. Sometimes, more severe injuries may require surgery, but these are unusual.

Knee injuries

Acute injuries to the knee are rare because most players wear kneepads. Sometimes, severe twists can result in torn knee ligaments that require surgery, but far more common is the overuse injury often referred to as jumper's knee.

Volleyball is tough on the hands, thumbs, and wrists. Careful taping, however, can usually take care of most hand injuries.

OVERUSE INJURIES

KNEES

Jumper's knee is a dull, aching pain usually located at the bottom of the kneecap. Technically known as patellar tendonitis, it is responsible for eighty percent of overuse injuries in volleyball. The more often you jump, and the more powerfully you jump, the more likely you are to suffer from it. Studies have shown that you are most likely to suffer if you are a jumper training hard to improve; if you bend your legs more than 90° when jumping; and if you have been playing competitively for between three and five years.

SHOULDER INJURIES

Shoulder tendonitis results from repeated sweeps of the arm above shoulder level and is also suffered by swimmers and tennis players. Spiking and serving are chiefly responsible for these injuries—particularly the floater serve, where the follow-through is held back, thus limiting the spin given to the ball. Symptoms include generalized pain in the shoulder area and a feeling of weakness in the shoulder.

LOWER BACK INJURIES

This general ache at the base of the spine results from serving and spiking. Much of the power for jump serving and spiking is generated in the lower back, and overexertion can lead to problems. Landing also jars the lower back. Over time, these two factors may combine to cause pain.

TREATMENT

Any acute injury triggers a three-stage response in the body:

- First, there is damage to the tissue—muscles or ligaments—which causes bleeding. In the more severe cases, this bleeding can be seen on the surface as bruising.

- Second, the body protects the damaged area by swelling and inflaming the area. This protects the area from further impacts and prevents any movement that could increase the damage.

- Third, the body begins to repair the damage that has been done. Two to three days after the injury occurs, new blood vessels begin to form around the damaged area. Three to five days later, new tissue—a scar—is formed.

Unlike the original undamaged tissue, scar tissue needs higher maintenance to remain supple. If it is not stretched and exercised regularly, especially during the healing process, scar tissue will shrink. This leaves the damaged area greatly reduced in flexibility and prone to stiffness.

LOWER SPINE

On landing, any impact that is not absorbed by the knees will be absorbed by the lower back.

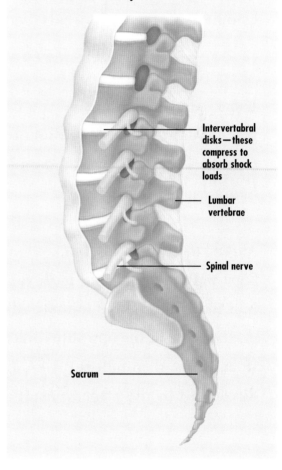

Intervertabral disks—these compress to absorb shock loads

Lumbar vertebrae

Spinal nerve

Sacrum

FOLLOWING A TREATMENT REGIME

Following is a sample plan for treating an injury to the ankle, the most common of acute injuries. First, follow the P.R.I.C.E. program. If you can walk without pain, do so. Otherwise, rest the injury completely for at least twenty-four hours.

AFTER ONE TO THREE DAYS

If the pain is lessening and you can walk, do so carefully. If you feel you can exercise gently, without too much pain, rock the foot slowly from heel to toe, then in and out. Try this for two minutes every three hours, but do not overdo it.

AFTER THREE TO EIGHT DAYS

Start walking more, and push your exercises a little further. Move your foot until you feel the injury pulling. Hold this for one second, then do the same in the opposite direction. Exercise for five minutes every three hours, then follow P.R.I.C.E. If you cannot walk without severe discomfort by this stage, consult a doctor.

P.R.I.C.E.
Protection

As soon as you feel an injury or any unexplained pain, you need to stop playing and get off the court as quickly as possible. Move to a place or position where you can take pressure off the injury.

AFTER NINE TO TWENTY-ONE DAYS

You should be moving more comfortably by now. However, start running only when you can stand on tiptoe and hop on the injured leg without pain. Until then, ride a bike or swim to stay in shape and keep your ankle limber.

Swimming is a gentle and effective way of regaining strength after injury, since it puts little stress on the muscles or ligaments and the water supports the body.

For stationary exercises, try crouching for a count of five, being careful to transfer the weight from the heels to the balls of the feet slowly. Next, stand with your feet shoulder-width apart. Then put your weight on your good leg and roll the other foot outward slowly, feeling the pull. Then balance on your injured leg, rising onto your toes for a count of five. Repeat each of these four times.

Rest

Let the pain settle before gently testing the injury. Can you move the joint without severe pain? If you can, keep manipulating the joint gently without causing yourself too much pain—keeping it flexible will help the healing process. If you cannot, keep the joint stationary because you will increase the damage by moving it. If the pain is especially bad, you will need to rest the joint completely for up to twenty-four hours.

Ice

Apply ice to the injury as soon as you can. This reduces inflammation, dulls the pain, and limits the damage to the soft tissue. Crushed ice should be placed in a plastic bag, then wrapped in a towel and wrapped around the injury. Applying ice directly can burn the skin. You can also use a bag of frozen peas wrapped in a towel. Apply ice for no longer than fifteen minutes. If the treatment is becoming painful, stop using ice therapy and use cold therapy instead.

Cold therapy is used for older and younger patients, whose skin is too fragile for ice therapy. Place small towels in a bucket of iced water, wring one out, and wrap it around the injury. Replace with a cold towel when the first towel warms up. You can also place hands or feet in the bucket, but check on them as above. Repeat ice or cold therapy every three hours. It is particularly effective after you have been exercising.

Compression

Using **compression bandages** to apply pressure to the injury will limit internal bleeding and swelling. Apply the bandage as soon as possible after the injury, but only after you have completed your first session of ice therapy. Make sure that the bandage provides pressure both above and below the injury area and is tight enough to be effective, but not so tight that it keeps blood from circulating.

Elevation

As soon as possible after the injury has been incurred, raise the injured area higher than your heart. This is done in order to limit bruising and swelling.

Elevation should be employed as often as possible and can be combined with ice therapy or compression.

TRAINING TO AVOID INJURY

Prevention is always better than cure. As far as acute injuries go, there is much you can do to keep yourself injury-free. Think about the injuries you have had and how they happened. Then plan your training schedule to address the areas in which you are weak.

Overuse injuries are very easily avoided—stop training. You may not have to stay off the court completely, though. Studies have shown that jumpers suffer the most overuse injuries, so the recommended course of action is—jump less! Working hard on jumping training makes little difference to the height you can reach or the power you develop. Good jumpers are good jumpers whether they train or not. If you train hard most days and feel your knees, shoulders, and lower back aching, you might consider changing games for a time, and play beach volleyball instead. You will still be enhancing your skills, but, statistically, you will be five times less likely to suffer injuries because sand is much more forgiving than a hard court.

Bandaging an injured joint as soon as possible will limit internal bleeding and shorten the recovery period.

A Career in Volleyball

Even a volleyball legend such as Karch Kiraly has to start somewhere, and, the younger you start, the sooner you can develop your potential. If you enjoy playing the game, get yourself some equipment and a good coach, and see how far you can go.

As well as being a professional sport, volleyball is also a great way to stay in shape and have fun. It is played everywhere—in gyms, backyards, parks, schoolyards, on beaches—and it requires hardly any equipment. All you need is a round ball to begin, and you can even practice passing without a net.

STARTING OUT

Some young people will know from a very early age that they are going to play volleyball seriously. For them, U.S.A. Volleyball runs a Youth Program called the United States Youth Volleyball League (www.usyvl.com). This program welcomes boys and girls aged eight to fourteen, and promises each of them a game and teaches the importance of FAST: Fun—Action—Skills—Teamwork. Parents can volunteer to help out as coaches, assistants, first-aiders, and administrators. A majority of states, however, still do not have a league set up.

A volleyball player jumps in the air as he sets the ball in a men's volleyball game at the 1990 Goodwill Games at the Hec Edmundson Pavilion, University of Washington, Seattle.

KARCH KIRALY

Karch Kiraly and Kent Steffes celebrate victory in the Olympic Games in Atlanta in 1996.

Karch Kiraly has been playing professional volleyball, both indoor and beach, for twenty years. Born in Jackson, Missouri, in 1960, Karch was still a young child when his father, Dr. Laszlo Kiraly, an immigrant from Hungary, moved the family to Santa Barbara, California. He played his first game of volleyball with his father when he was just six.

As an international player of the indoor game, Karch won gold medals in the 1984 and 1988 Olympic Games, gold in the 1985 World Cup, 1986 World Champions, and gold in the 1987 Pan American Games. After achieving everything there was to achieve in indoor volleyball, Karch moved onto the beach. He won the King of the Beach tournament from 1991–1993 and again in 1996.

Karch has won beach titles with twelve different players. From 1993–96, he and teammate Kent Steffes racked up seventy-six titles. With new teammate Adam Johnson, the success continued. In 1999, the pairing won the Chicago Open and Kiraly's title record hit 140, making Kiraly the most successful beach volleyball player ever.

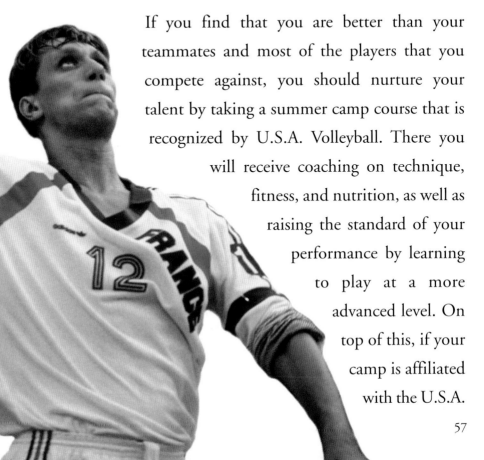

The original "King of the Beach," Sinjin Smith, and his teammate, Randy Stoklos, provide masterclass camps in beach volleyball for anyone eight years or older, at State Beach in Pacific Palisades, California. Kiraly himself is associated with the Starlings Volleyball Club program, aimed at bringing the benefits of playing volleyball to girls aged nine and over from underprivileged backgrounds.

For those who decide that they want to play the sport seriously, rather than just have fun with it, most high schools have teams of some sort.

If you find that you are better than your teammates and most of the players that you compete against, you should nurture your talent by taking a summer camp course that is recognized by U.S.A. Volleyball. There you will receive coaching on technique, fitness, and nutrition, as well as raising the standard of your performance by learning to play at a more advanced level. On top of this, if your camp is affiliated with the U.S.A.

Even if you don't make it as a professional player, you can still use your enthusiasm for volleyball to help make the sport more popular.

Giba of Brazil for once gets the better of the game's best blocker — the United States' Lloy Ball — during the 2002 World Volleyball Championships in Cordoba, Argentina.

Volleyball Talent Identification Program, your coach will be acting as a scout for U.S.A. Volleyball, identifying the best young talent in the country for special training. The coach will also have contacts with colleges throughout the country that are geared to volleyball.

Most of America's top sports talent emerges from colleges where intensive courses develop talented youths into professional athletes. However, attending college is expensive, and, if you need financial assistance, there are many scholarships for which you can apply.

COLLEGE VOLLEYBALL

First, you need to find a college that specializes in volleyball. Most colleges offer such courses (www.collegeview.com/college/collegesearch), but certain colleges produce players of the highest caliber. The reputation of individual colleges rises and falls as coaches come and go, but there are some colleges that will always provide an environment that encourages excellence in this sport. Right now, the best such colleges are Stanford University, Penn State University, California State University (Long Beach), University of Hawaii, and University of California at Los Angeles (U.C.L.A.) for women; and Brigham Young University, Pepperdine University, U.C.L.A., Hawaii, and Penn State for men.

The country's best college teams compete for honors in the **NCAA** (National Collegiate Athletic Association) championships. The national coaches will select from this highest college level the players that they want to represent the country in the All-American team.

Players such as Lloy Ball and Karch Kiraly are two of the finest athletes ever to represent their country. While not every volleyball player may go on to reach this elite level, there are many other options available, including numerous professional teams, an even greater number of regional teams, and hundreds of amateur teams. All of these teams naturally need players, coaching staff, and support staff, so there are many opportunities for a career in volleyball, even if you are not Karch Kiraly.

Glossary

Acute injury: Injuries caused by a single, traumatic event.

Aerobic: Exercise that demands increased oxygen and so forces the heart and breathing rates up.

Attack: To hit the ball across the net in order to win a rally.

Attack line: Two lines, one in either court, both parallel to the net and 10 feet (3 m) either side of it.

Back line setter: The ball is "set" by one of the players in the back line, who lobs it towards the net to set up an attack; one of the players near the net then attacks the ball.

Back row attack: Attack delivered by a player behind the attack line.

Block: Defensive maneuver by one or more players, aimed at keeping the ball from crossing the net and winning a point.

Bump (v.): To make a short-range forearm pass.

Buddy taping: Strapping an injured finger to the uninjured finger next to it.

Compression bandage: A bandage that holds a swollen joint or muscle tightly in order to reduce the swelling.

Dink: A soft-handed shot made with fingertips.

FIVB: The abbreviation for the *Fédération Internationale de Volleyball*, the sport's governing body, now based in Switzerland.

Floater: A serve hit with no follow through and no spin.

Forearm pass: A pass made with the arms straight and hands together, by moving the shoulders to hit the ball just above the wrists.

Hamstrings: The group of three muscles set at the back of the thigh.

Hitter: The player delivering the attacking shot.

Inversion: An acute injury, usually resulting in some degree of sprain, where the ankle rolls over the outside of the foot.

Joust: This is when two players are contesting the ball at the net and it becomes held between the opposing players' hands. The referee can have the point replayed.

NCAA: Abbreviation for the National Collegiate Athletic Association, the organization that establishes sports rules and regulations for colleges.

Overpronate (v.): A tendency for the arch of the foot to collapse inward to an excessive degree when taking a step.

Overuse injury: An injury that results from repetitive physical maneuvers performed over a long period of time.

P.R.I.C.E.: An acronym for the common method of treating non-serious sprains and strains—Protection, Rest, Ice, Compression, Elevation.

Quadriceps: The large four-part muscle on the front of each thigh, used to extend the leg.

Rotate/rotation: One-position clockwise movement of players through the serving position and around the court.

Serve: Starting play by delivering the ball into the opposing court from the back right position.

Set (v.): To position the ball so the hitter can make an attacking shot.

Setter: The player who receives the pass and sets up the attack.

Spike (v.): To make a powerful, high-speed attacking shot.

Substitution: Replacing one player with another for tactical or performance reasons; fifteen are allowed per game.

UV rays: Ultraviolet rays, a type of damaging radiation in sunlight.

Further Information

USEFUL WEB SITES

For more about Beach volleyball, visit the California Beach Volleyball
Association's web site: www.cbva.org

For more information about college athletics, you can browse the web site for
the National Collegiate Athletic Association (NCAA): www.ncaa.org

U.S.A. Volleyball: www.usavolleyball.org

The Web sites listed on this page were active at the time of publication. The publisher is not
responsible for Web sites that have changed their address or discontinued operation since the
date of publication. The publisher will review and update the Web sites upon each reprint.

FURTHER READING

American Sport Education Program. *Coaching Youth Volleyball*. Champaign,
Illinois: Human Kinetics, 2001.

Kiraly, Karch. *Beach Volleyball*. Champaign, Illinois: Human Kinetics, 1999.

Scales, Al and Mike Linn. *Complete Conditioning for Volleyball*. Champaign,
Illinois: Human Kinetics, 2002.

Shondell, Don and Cecile Reynaud. *Volleyball Coaching Bible*. Champaign,
Illinois: Human Kinetics, 2002.

Wise, Mary. *Volleyball Drills for Champions*. Champaign, Illinois: Human
Kinetics, 1998.

THE AUTHOR

Chris Beeson is a London-based photojournalist with a degree in psychology and a long-held interest in the psychology of sports performance. As well as sailing at World Championship level, he has played many sports at a regional representative level, including soccer, volleyball (indoor and beach), and basketball. He now works as a motivational coach and consultant for several sports and fitness clubs.

THE CONSULTANTS

Susan Saliba, Ph.D., is a senior associate athletic trainer and a clinical instructor at the University of Virginia in Charlottesville, Virginia. A certified athletic trainer and licensed physical therapist, Dr. Saliba provides sports medicine care, including prevention, treatment, and rehabilitation for the varsity athletes at the University. Dr. Saliba holds dual appointments as an Assistant Professor in the Curry School of Education and the Department of Orthopaedic Surgery. She is a member of the National Athletic Trainers' Association's Educational Executive Committee and its Clinical Education Committee.

Eric Small, M.D., a Harvard-trained sports medicine physician, is a nationally recognized expert in the field of sports injuries, nutritional supplements, and weight management programs. He is author of *Kids & Sports* (2002) and is Assistant Clinical Professor of Pediatrics, Orthopedics, and Rehabilitation Medicine at Mount Sinai School of Medicine in New York. He is also Director of the Sports Medicine Center for Young Athletes at Blythedale Children's Hospital in Valhalla, New York. Dr. Small has served on the American Academy of Pediatrics Committee on Sports Medicine for the past six years, where he develops national policy regarding children's medical issues and sports.

Index